Lord, Teach Us to Pray!

THE
LORD'S
PRAYER

SERMONS ON THE LORD'S PRAYER

GORDON KENWORTHY REED

LORD, TEACH US TO PRAY!
by Gordon Kenworthy Reed

Copyright © 2016 by Tanglewood Publishing

ISBN-13: 978-0-9972490-0-2

Tanglewood Publishing

800-241-4016

fortressbk@aol.com

TANGLEWOOD
PUBLISHING

Cover Layout and Design by Sara Renick/Indigenous Images
Book Design and Layout by Mieke Moller

Printed in the United States of America

OUR FATHER,

WHICH ART IN HEAVEN,

HALLOWED BE THY NAME.

THY KINGDOM COME.

THY WILL BE DONE IN EARTH,

AS IT IS IN HEAVEN.

GIVE US THIS DAY OUR DAILY BREAD.

AND FORGIVE US OUR TRESPASSES,

AS WE FORGIVE THEM THAT TRESPASS AGAINST US.

AND LEAD US NOT INTO TEMPTATION,

BUT DELIVER US FROM EVIL.

FOR THINE IS THE KINGDOM,

THE POWER, AND THE GLORY,

for ever and ever. Amen.

TABLE OF CONTENTS

INTRODUCTION

REFERENCES

INTRODUCTION

The Lord's Prayer was given as a pattern and example for prayer to the disciples of Jesus, and through them to the Christian Church of all ages. It is the most often used prayer, and most frequently quoted passage from the Bible. However, it is seldom used in the way in which Christ meant for us to use it. Of this, I am convinced. It is very proper and profitable for use as a public prayer in a gathering of Christians, but this is not the primary use for which it was intended. This prayer is the most comprehensive and the most concise of all prayers. It speaks to every need of man, and tells of all which he may expect from God. If a believer will master this prayer and its meaning, he will know how to pray. He will be able to "enter into his room alone, and shut the door and pray to his Father in heaven, and his Father who sees him in secret will reward him openly."[1]

It is surprising and alarming to realize that there is very little practical help available to Christians in their understanding and proper use of this prayer. To be sure there are tools which the student of the Bible may use. There are some commentaries available that offer help, but there is little in the way of readily available, easily understood material on this subject.

The printing of this series of sermons is offered in the hope that this might help to fill the vacancy for you. In order for you to get the most possible benefit from these sermons, let me suggest a simple preparatory exercise before you read them. You probably know that I never preach a sermon without first praying that God the Holy Spirit will speak through my words, and that He will help you to hear and understand what He would say. Before you begin any or all of these sermons, let me suggest that you too join in this prayer, and ask God to speak to your heart. In this way you will not only capture something of the spirit in which these sermons were prepared and preached, but you will also be claiming the promise of Jesus, "Ask, and it will be given you, seek and you will find, knock, and it will be opened unto you."[2]

1

INCREASING YOUR FAITH

There is nothing that reveals a person's spiritual health so much as the state and status of his prayer life. Not his ability to pray in public, even the act of leading in public prayer, but his own personal, private fellowship with the Lord by himself, and alone. Prayer is not only the ultimate test of our spiritual condition, but is the highest and most important activity of the soul. Prayer is our greatest need, and at the same time our greatest and most frequent failure is our failure to pray. One of our problems is that we really do not know how to pray, or for what things we should pray. The Lord's Prayer fills this gap and tells us generally and specifically how to pray and for what things. It includes everything we need to know about prayer. It is in itself an answer to prayer. It was given at the request (prayer) of Jesus' disciples, "Lord, teach us to pray." This is how Jesus taught us to pray. You do not have to pray this way, but before you decide your way is better, just remember that Jesus was the perfect Revealer of the Father; in fact, He is *the* Revelation of God to man. So this is how God invites us to come into His presence and to make our requests known.

It is not enough just to say the words of this prayer and nothing more. Jesus said, "After this *manner* pray." These are the things which Jesus thought important, and this is the way He knew was the right way to come to the Father. If we master this prayer, and understand its full meaning; if we will truly learn to pray in this manner, then we will know God. He will bless us. All the infinite resources of heaven will be placed at our disposal. Our faith will increase, and we will develop a living, vital contact between heaven and earth. In this particular sermon, we will concern ourselves just with the address of the prayer, "Our Father, which (or who) art in heaven."

"Our Father." What a bold, audacious way for sinful man to address the living God. No man has this right, unless it be given him by God. Let us be very clear at this point. Remember it was Jesus who taught us this prayer, and He said, "No man comes to the Father but by me."[1] The right to call God "our Father" is a gift of Jesus Christ to those who love and trust Him as their Saviour. He was, and is, the only begotten Son of the Father, but the Father has given Him the right and power to call men to Him that they might become the sons of God through faith in Jesus. Not every man hears or accepts this gift. No one ever drew the line of distinction more sharply than did Jesus. He continually reminded His disciples that some did not and would not receive Him, and therefore could not know God as their Father. He said of certain ones who self righteously opposed Him at every turn, "Ye are of your father, the devil."[2] He ever reminded His disciples of the coming day of final separation that would forever divide men, some to be forever with their Father in heaven; others forever dispelled from His presence.

So as soon as we begin the Lord's Prayer by saying "Our Father," we are to pause and consider, is He our Father? Have I personally claimed His Son as my Saviour that I might truly call him Father? And we are also to say these words with a profound sense of gratitude and love for this precious gift.

Anyone may say these words with his lips, but how many can say them from the heart? Those of us who have accepted His Son, and thus have been born again and adopted into God's family, we too must stop and think, are we living as children of God or as children of this world? Is there anything about my life that distinguishes me from other men? God refuses to be called Father by those who reject His Son, whether this rejection be outright refusal of His grace, or simply an insincere profession that is not proven by life.

Once this issue is settle, and once we know that we are in Christ Jesus by His grace, then we can turn to God, as our Father, and know that He loves us and cares for us. We can be assured that He is more eager to bless us than we are to receive His blessing. We feel confident that nothing can separate us from the love of God. We can know that our sins have been forgiven, removed from us "as far as the east is from the west,"[3] and "cast into the depths of the sea."[4] We know that we can trust Him with the keeping of our souls. We can also know that when life no longer is pleasant and good, and when there is nothing left in this world for us, that we have a Father, and therefore we have a home and a hope.

We pray "Our Father" but we do not stop there, we pray "Our Father, who art in heaven." This qualifying phrase, if you may call it that, adds richness and depth to our understanding of God. He is our Father, but He is not a God who we can have for our own purposes. He is the Almighty, the Everliving and Everlasting God of eternity. He is not a good luck charm or magic potion that can be used as men wish. He is far above all our ideas and notions of earthly fatherhood.

It is not enough to call him Father and let it go at that. If that is all we can say about God, what will the small child think whose father is a drunken tyrant? What will he think of God when he sees his mother abused and beaten, and when he himself becomes the innocent victim of his father's mad rage? No, there is more that may be said of God, and indeed must be said of Him. We address Him as "Our Father in heaven" because He knows all about us; past, present, and future. As the scripture says, "All things are naked and open before the eyes of Him with whom we have to do."[5] He knows every need and every sin before you ask for blessing or forgiveness.

If you want the blessing of God, it is absolutely necessary that you be honest with yourself and with Him. Nothing is hidden from God. He has the power to punish and to bless. A little girl, who like the little girl in the nursery rhyme had been "horrid" all day long, was being put to bed by her father. She would not say her prayers, because in her childish anger she was mad at the whole world and God too. Her father said her prayers for her and as he tucked her in and kissed her good night, he saw the tears running down her face and her lips trembling with hurt and anger. In his prayer he had asked God to forgive her for her sins, and she blurted out, "Why did you have to go and tell God on me?" Childish? Of course, but no more childish than our refusal to be absolutely honest in our prayers to our heavenly Father who knows all about even our inner secret thoughts and attitudes. A man with a serious drinking problem overheard his wife praying, "O God, have mercy on my poor drunken husband." He burst into her room shouting, "Don't tell him I'm drunk, tell him I'm sick!" Once again, the foolishness of being anything but open and honest with God.

He is a great and able God to whom you come when you pray "Our Father who art in heaven." He is able to do far "abundantly above all you can ask or think."[6] He knows how to perform His will for you. He knows just what answer to give to your prayer that is best for you, and He has the power to do it.

So when you pray, remember you pray to the Holy, Almighty, and Powerful God, who in Christ Jesus has become your Father in heaven, who loves you and knows you as a good father loves and knows his children. The perfect God loves you with a perfect love. Every need you have is known to Him before you request His help. Every tear that falls from your eyes is known by Him and is felt by Him. He hears every weary sigh, every inward groaning. He wants to help you. He waits for you with eager arms of love. He has given you His Son. Will He not also freely give you all things? When you pray, be still and know that He is God. Before you confess a single sin, before you ask for even one blessing for yourself or others, call upon Him who is your Father in heaven. Be aware that you are in His presence, rejoice in Him and be glad.

When you pray, say "Our Father who art in heaven."

2

Hallowed Be Thy Name

The Lord's Prayer is truly the perfect prayer. In it we have the pattern which guides in all prayer. It is perfect both in its content and order, but it is also perfect because the One who gave it to us was Himself perfect. It is well to pause and consider to whom this prayer was given. It was given to men who were disciples (followers) of Jesus Christ, who wanted to know how to pray. Do you want a strong prayer life? Do you want the blessing of God in your life? Do you want to know how to "stay in touch" with God? Then learn this prayer. Master its every detail, explore its inner meaning, and these blessings will be yours.

One of the great lessons which this prayer teaches, and one which we tend to ignore, is the order of the Lord's Prayer. In this prayer, first things come first, and each part logically follows what comes before and precedes what comes after. In this great prayer, and especially in the opening words, the focus is not upon the needs of man, but upon the greatness of God.

This is what Jesus taught us. When you pray, think first of God. Remember that through Christ Jesus He has become your Father, that He is Holy and Almighty. Therefore, He is your first concern in prayer, that you may know and adore Him for Himself. The first petition of the Lord's Prayer, "Hallowed be thy name," speaks of this first concern. Let us now explore together what we mean when we pray, "Hallowed be thy name."

This is a prayer for the knowledge of God.

By this petition we pray that all men might truly know God as He is, and understand the Revelation which He has given of Himself. We pray also that men might realize their need of Him, and seek Him. How little do we yearn and pray for men to know God! How little do we know Him! What false and faulty concepts of God we build up in our minds! We continually seek to create God in our image, and make Him conform to our ideas. How foolish. How sinful. The human mind is by nature a manufacturer of idols and false gods.

Jesus knew this, and His purpose was to reveal the true God, the Father, to the world. His burning desire and passion was to make God known to men. He wished for His disciples to know the Father, even as He knew Him, in all His fullness, beauty, and glory.

The Bible tells us of God who is our Creator and our Redeemer. It tells us that God is our Righteousness, our Peace, our Rock and Fortress. He is revealed as the Good Shepherd who satisfies the wants of His people. He is shown to be the God who provides for His own. He is the God of the Covenant. So when we pray, "Hallowed by they name," we pray that we and all men might come to know Him in these ways in which He has revealed Himself. We pray that we may experience this kind of relationship with Him, and that all might join us in this experience.

The Psalmist calls to us, "O magnify the Lord with me, and let us exalt His name together."[1] We cannot add to the greatness of God; we cannot add to the glory of His name. But we can share in the mission of revealing the greatness of God to the world. We can do this through our word of witness. We can do this through lives that reflect the love of God and His glorious attributes. A believer, a Christian, is one who bears the name of his Saviour God (Christian), and accepts the responsibility of bearing that name in the world. So when we pray "Hallowed be thy name" we are praying for God to use us to this end. How serious is this prayer, how awesome, how inspiring! Just think, the Christian himself is, in part, the answer to this petition. We dare not pray these words lightly, with no thought to their meaning, or no sense of personal responsibility.

This is a prayer for the reverence of God.

Not only do we pray that men might know God in the truth of His revelation, but that He may be loved, admired, adored, and reverenced throughout the whole earth. We are guilty of being so glib and irreverent when we speak the name of God. The proliferation of profanity has reached alarming proportions. Perhaps we need an experience such as Isaiah had at the beginning of his prophetic ministry.[2] He was depressed because of the death of the great King Uzziah, and all the insecurity which change inevitably brings. He was overcome because of the decline of true religion in Israel, and the wildfire spread of evil. He needed reassurance as he sought for the Lord in His temple.

God always answers beyond our prayers and thought. When Isaiah entered the temple he had a life-changing, glorious vision of God. He saw the Lord upon His throne high and lifted up above the earth. He saw the Mighty Angels who waited before Him, too bright and beautiful for human eyes to see or words to describe, yet who before the presence of the Lord worshiped in great humility, daring not to look upon Him or set their feet on the ground in His presence. Isaiah was overwhelmed. His heart condemned him in the presence of such Mighty Purity and Holiness, and he bewailed his own sin and the sins of his people. He prayed for a clean heart and clean lips. When one reads through the Book of Isaiah, one finds the imprint of that vision stamped indelibly upon the man and the book. His writings contain some of the most majestic and lofty ideas of God that are ever revealed. Along with this sense of reverence, there is also a painful awareness of man's sin.

One of the great sins of our age, even among those known as Christians, is the lack of reverence for God and His great holy Name. This is because we do not know Him as we should. We have attempted to reduce Him to our level. We only have to take seriously His self-revelation in the Scriptures to gain a new sense of awe and reverence. Reverence for God is the key to concern for others and contentment within. Reverence for God leads to a greater and more holy love for Him, just for Himself and not for fear of hell or hope of heaven. Perhaps you have heard of the legend of the angel who appeared to a saint in her dreams. The angel bore in one hand a shell filled with water, and in the other, a great curtain. When asked by the saint for the meaning of the vision, the angel replied, "The water is to extinguish the fires of hell, the curtain to cover the beauty of heaven, that men might learn to love God for himself alone."

God is holy, His name is sacred, and it is for our good and blessing that we hold it so.

This is a prayer for the glory of God.

Everything we ask from God should be tempered by this first petition, and in harmony with it. Whatever may be our request, however deeply we may feel the need of it, we must first stop and think, "Is this for God's glory?" For Jesus, this was always His first concern, that He might glorify His Father. Even in His hour of great agony and personal need, when all alone as He prayed in the Garden of Gethsemane, His first concern was for the will and glory of His Father. Now maybe we can begin to see why so much of our praying is so empty, so powerless, so futile, so unrewarding. One of the true signs of a redeemed soul is the primary concern for the glory of God in life. A Christian, by his very nature, must seek first the kingdom of God and must also seek above all other goals to glorify his Lord.

There is a very real sense in which all prayer must be directed to this end. When we are praying for ourselves, we must ask for His glory in our lives and must ask for all things only that they may result in His glory. When we pray for others, the petitions we ask for them must be hallowed by this same desire. We pray for the sick and ask that they be healed if it is for God's glory and their good.

When we pray, "Hallowed by thy name," we pray in great hope. We know that our Lord has promised that one day "every knee shall bow and every tongue confess that Christ is Lord, to the glory of God the Father."[3] So we pray for the coming of that day through this petition.

> *When you pray therefore, say,*
> *"Our Father who art in heaven,*
> *hallowed by thy name."*

3

THY KINGDOM COME

Man is a dreamer of dreams. He is a hopeless dreamer. One of the universal dreams of all men everywhere has been the dream of a golden age for the human race. Some like to hark back to the good days (which really never were that good). Others speak of a coming age of peace and perfection. Men have written their dreams down for all to read. They have written of a Utopia, of a perfect Republic, and ideal Kingdom, a hidden Shangri-la. Because man is what he is, he must yearn for a dream of such things.

There is a definite concrete reality behind the dreams of man. It is the Kingdom of God. It is the kingdom foretold by the prophets and proclaimed by Christ and His disciples. In its final and complete form it is the fulfillment of all that for which man hopes and dreams. It will be a kingdom of righteousness, of security, of peace and joy, of fulfillment and perfection. In the words of the prayer which Christ taught His disciples, the hopes and dreams of man become the prayer of the Christian, "Thy kingdom come."

Once again, as in previous sermons on this prayer, let me stress the importance of understanding the logical order of this prayer. We begin by addressing the great God of heaven as our Father. We adore and worship Him both as Almighty God and ever-loving Father. Our first concern is for His glory and His honor as we pray, "Hallowed be they name." Immediately upon so praying, we pray, "Thy kingdom come." We are still in the part of the Lord's Prayer that puts the things of God uppermost in our minds. His concerns are greater and vastly more important than ours. Praying for the coming of His kingdom is a part of what is involved in "seeking first the kingdom of God and His righteousness."[1]

The burden of much of Christ's preaching and teaching was the kingdom of God. His first public proclamation was, "Repent and believe, for the kingdom of heaven is at hand."[2] Many of His parables, indeed most of them, were concerning the kingdom. His last act on earth just before He died was to receive one into His kingdom. The dying thief prayed, "Lord, remember me when Thou comest into Thy kingdom." In response to that prayer, Jesus said, "Today thou shalt be with me in paradise."[3]

We cannot pray, "Thy kingdom come" with any understanding or fervency unless we understand the term, "The kingdom of God." What is it? In what sense can we pray for its coming? The simplest answer to the question is that the kingdom of God is the rule of God in the lives of men. This definition may be expanded and expounded to include factors of extent, time, and degree, but basically the kingdom of God is a relationship between man and God.

The Kingdom of God now in this present world.

The prayer, "Thy kingdom come" is a prayer for things in the present tense. We pray for God to extend His kingdom into the hearts and lives of men everywhere, beginning with ourselves. Thus this is a missionary prayer. It should ever be on the hearts and lips of believers. By this prayer we acknowledge that the kingdom can only come by Divine initiative. We cannot bring in the kingdom, we cannot make it happen. Only God can cause His kingdom to come in men. Just as only the second coming of Christ will bring His kingdom to fulfillment, so even now only the coming of Christ into a person's heart can effect the rule of God there. In Calvin's catechism the question is posed, "In what sense do you pray that His kingdom may come?" Calvin's answer reads, "That day by day the Lord may increase the number of faithful, that day by day He may increasingly bestow His graces upon them, until He has fulfilled them completely..."

When we pray, "Thy kingdom come," we long for these things to be accomplished. We pray for the success of the Gospel, for the conversion of the lost. There is a certain way in which men enter the kingdom. The Bible is quite plain at this point. To enter the kingdom, men must repent of their sins. In old Athens, among the many temples which graced the ancient city, two in particular are interesting at this point. They stood together, the temple of virtue and the temple of honor. The only way in which one could enter the temple of honor was through the temple of virtue. So it is with the kingdom; men may only enter through repentance.

Added to repentance is the necessity of humility. Jesus said, "Except ye be converted and become as little children, ye shall in no wise enter the kingdom."[4] Humility is required of those who enter. We must humble ourselves before God and cast aside pride and self, and trusting fully His mercy and grace, enter in.

Faith is the other requirement. We can only become God's children, and thus citizens of the kingdom, by faith in Jesus Christ as Lord and Saviour. So as we pray this prayer, we are praying that we and others might experience these things and come into His kingdom. God's part is the gift of the new birth and acceptance.

The Kingdom in conflict.

The Kingdom of God is a present reality in this world, but not all accept the offer. The Kingdom is in conflict with the powers of darkness and sin. Men refuse both King and Kingdom. There are many reasons for this. Some men fear the cost of entering the Kingdom. There is nothing easy about repentance, humility, and faith. Jesus spoke of denying ourselves, taking up the cross, and following Him. This frightens some. Others are too engrossed in the affairs and cares of this world. Far too many people have made the possession of things, riches, and power their god and their kingdom. Of course, we cannot overlook the active, violent opposition of Satan to the things of God. Sin rules the heart of natural man. Paul spoke of Satan as being the "God of this world."[5] God and His kingdom are in constant conflict, even within your life.

When we pray, "Thy kingdom come," we are aware of this conflict, and pray for the overthrow of evil generally and specifically. This is no easy task. The Christian has an obligation to join sides in this war. Neutrality is impossible. Personally it can be a dangerous prayer. Do you really want the overthrow of evil within you? Do you really want to give up your pride and greed, your evil thoughts, and hasty tongue? To pray "Thy kingdom come" in a personal way leads to upheaval, disruption, and change in your life. Are you prepared to face that?

One aspect of this prayer concerns the church. The Christian should continually, fervently, pray for the church of Jesus Christ on earth. He should pray for his own church, his own denomination, but never stop there. We should all pray for the whole church. We should pray for our oppressed brothers behind the iron curtain and the bamboo curtain. We should remember them with tears and "groanings which cannot be uttered."

The Kingdom of God eternal, triumphant.

This great prayer is answered every time a sinner repents, at every triumph of truth, every victory of right, no matter how small or great. But the final answer to this prayer is found in none of these things. This prayer has an eternal dimension. Simon Peter said, "We are looking for and hastening to the coming day of the Lord..."[6] Our prayer is not only for a spiritual, unseen kingdom, but for a visible, personal, and powerful coming of the Lord from heaven. We pray that "The kingdoms of this world will become the kingdom of our Lord..." Not until then, when sin, death, pain, sorrow, wrong, and all enemies of the soul are defeated, will this prayer be answered.

When Jesus was eating the last Passover Supper with His disciples, and thus beginning the first "Lord's Supper," He said that He would not drink again of the fruit of the vine with them until He drank it new in His Father's kingdom.[7] This blessed sacrament is not only a look and a link with the past, but a pledge that one day the kingdom will come. All dreams and prayers will be fulfilled. In the days of the exile of Prince Charles of Scotland, there was never a gathering of highlanders without the lifting of the cup in pledge of the return of their prince and king. So when we lift the cup and break the bread, we do so until He comes again in His glory and kingdom.

By this we are encouraged when we pray to say,
"...thy kingdom come..."

4

THY WILL BE DONE IN EARTH AS IT IS IN HEAVEN

When one of the greater Puritan ministers lay dying, his last words were, "Lord, what thou wilt, where thou wilt, and how thou wilt." In these words he expressed not only his faith, but an apt summary of his entire life. When we pray this part of the Lord's Prayer, "Thy will be done," we are praying a prayer that will always be answered. God is Sovereign. He rules and over-rules in all things, in all places. In the drama of human history, He is the leading actor, and all men, no matter how great or small, play but a supporting role to Him.

There is another sense in which this prayer is not being an-swered, not yet at any rate. There is so much in the world that opposes God and is contrary to His will. The story begins with sin and continues through all its fruit. There is so much hatred, so many wars, so much violence, infidelity to truth, private and public immorality, the pollution of our environment, and the more deadly pollution of the minds of people. No, we cannot say that God's will is being done perfectly on earth today.

The beauty of the Lord's Prayer must not blind us to its first use; that is a guide to learning how to pray. This petition is the next step following the prayer, "Thy kingdom come." God's kingdom is the sphere in which the will of God is being done; therefore, it naturally follows that once we pray for the coming of His kingdom, we should pray for the accomplishment of His will. On the other hand, we dare not begin to pray for our wants and needs (Give us our daily bread, forgive us our debts, etc.) until we learn to truly pray, "Thy will be done." As in each part of the Lord's Prayer, there is an unending wealth of riches and wisdom in these words, "Thy will be done."

This prayer is an affirmation of faith.

I see first in this petition a great affirmation of faith. This is our firm belief, our cherished conviction, our living experience with God. We believe in the power and authority of God, and we categorically deny that either chance or evil control. We believe in the providence of God that is actively at work, over-ruling the wrath and sin of man to the glory of God. Though evil may seem in control, it *only* seems so. In the final sense we can never accept this illusion. God is God alone. This is the only life view that makes sense or that can save us from utter despair. Wordsworth once said, "One adequate support for the calamities of life exists, one only: an assured belief that the procession of our fate, however bad or disturbed, is ordered by a Being of infinite goodness and power."

The Christian believes that every joy or sorrow, every victory or defeat is all a part of the often mysterious but always loving plan and purpose of God for the life of His child. This does not mean we surrender to apathy or adopt a fatalistic attitude, or that we become cowards, not at all. Rather we believe this is what the Bible means when it says, "The just shall live by faith."[1] We cannot always account for the happenings which occur, and which at the moment may seem so strange, so inconvenient, but we can believe that God is at work in all things to accomplish His good purpose. John Calvin went through Geneva on his way to Italy by sheer accident (or so it seemed). He had no plans to remain beyond the next dawn, but God had other plans for Calvin, for a life of service which still deeply influences the world.

This prayer is an act of commitment.

When we pray, "Thy will be done," we are engaging in a personal act of dedication and commitment with tremendous significance. We are saying in effect, "I will seek to know God's will for my life, and I will pledge myself to fulfill it." This means a surrender of self. It means forsaking sin, even the most cherished and most deeply ingrained ones that have become a part of our personalities. This means also a re-adjusting of priorities. We have no right to pray this prayer, "Thy will be done" unless by these words we mean to say "in me." The idea is that we should present our bodies as living sacrifices unto God, wholly acceptable, which is our reasonable service. This is a prayer that God would break us, melt us, mold, us, fill us, and use us. Martin Luther prayed, "O Father, let me not fall so low that my will may be done. Break my will, put obstacles in the way, that come what may, not my will but Thine be done."

Are you willing to pray from your heart, "Thy will be done?" It is easy enough to say these words in general, but when we are

put to a particular test, we can still pray willingly, eagerly, "Thy
will be done." Is there even one area in your life in which you
are unwilling to pray this prayer? If so, then you cannot pray it
at all.

A dear friend of mine, who is the father of three wonderful girls,
was bereaved of his only son several years back. The child was
born with a defective heart, and it soon became apparent that
the young boy could not live beyond infancy. This good man,
who was only a young Christian at the time, struggled in ag-
onizing prayer for many days over his son. He was unwilling
to pray, "Thy will be done," but could only pray, "Dear Father,
spare and heal my son." Finally, after much mental and spiritual suffering on his part, and much physical suffering on the part
of the baby boy, the distraught father entered the hospital room
in which his son lay fretting and suffering, and dropped to his
knees with the simple prayer, "Thy will be done." He testified
that such a profound sense of peace flooded his soul that he had
never known such joy. Relief came as he had never experienced
before. He knew God was very close. When he opened his eyes
and arose from his knees, his infant son was safe in the arms of
Jesus, his suffering forever ended, and both father and son were
at peace.

Maybe some of you have experienced such things. The one
great example of self-surrender in these words, "Thy will be
done" is found in Jesus' experience in the Garden of Gethsemane.[2] Here is our example; here is the strength by which we
may pray this prayer.

This prayer is an ideal longed for.

This petition taught us by the Lord is not complete until we add, "...on earth as it is in heaven." This is a look by faith towards a sure and certain future. This petition contains this eternal dimension. Although it points us to a future age, still it has a very definite bearing on the present. An ideal with no hope of fulfillment is an empty illusion, but an ideal with certainty of fulfillment becomes a powerful motivating force. We cannot be satisfied with less than the perfect, the ideal. We pray for the perfections of heaven to be at work in our lives now.

A great artist who was known as a perfectionist said that he never achieved with his hand what his mind imagined, and that to him this was proof of heaven, the perfect kingdom of God. Our prayer, "Thy will be done on earth as it is in heaven," is an affirmation of faith, and act of commitment, but it is an expression of an ideal that will be surely fulfilled when God will have created the new heaven and new earth wherein dwells righteousness (perfection). We pray this prayer as those who realize that we are even now in preparation and training for that glorious wonderful age and place in which the perfect will of God will be perfectly done.

> *Therefore when you pray, say,*
> *"Our Father who art in heaven,*
> *hallowed be thy name.*
> *Thy kingdom come,*
> *thy will be done*
> *in earth as it is in heaven..."*

5

GIVE US THIS DAY OUR DAILY BREAD

Have you ever prayed, "Give us this day our daily bread" without really knowing where your next meal was coming from? Perhaps there are a few of you in this place today who can still remember the grim days of the Depression, and when you really did not know how you were going to eat or to feed your family from day to day, but very few of you have ever faced such a crisis. Do you realize that all over the world today there are Christian people, your brothers in Christ, who pray this prayer with faith, and yet who are hungry and have little prospect of improving their lot? Have you forgotten that in the lost wilderness of Siberia and inland China there are still countless thousands who have disappeared from civilization, languishing in inhuman concentration camps, many of whom are believers, and who constantly pray, "Give us our bread?"

Several years ago I was talking with a man who ministered in a city mission in one of our large southern cities. He was telling me of the early days of the mission when there were no funds to support the work. He said that many times he sat men down at tables for a meal without knowing where he would get food to put on the tables. Often these men would join this saintly minister (who had given up a comfortable city church and an important executive position that he might work with the "bums" and "castoffs" of society) in prayer for food when there was none in the mission pantry. The point of the story, however, is that they never missed even one meal! Some produce dealer would bring by the leftovers of the day, or a baker would send out his day-old bread, or a church would bring by a shower of food, but never once did the prayer, "Give us this day our daily bread" go unanswered.

In the Lord's Prayer there is an almost abrupt transition from the lofty things of God and His kingdom down to the common, everyday needs of man. Some might expect the Lord to deal first with the needs of the spirit, with forgiveness and cleansing, but this is not the case. The Lord was being perfectly logical and consistent in this petition. After all, the spirit resides within a human body, and the body must be fed and its needs met. There could be no piety or dedication without food for the body. There could be no act of worship, no self-denying gift, no winning of even one soul for Christ unless the body is maintained. There are other petitions immediately following this one which will remind us that man does not live by bread alone, and that the needs of the soul must be dealt with too, but just now our attention is turned to the request that God will supply our physical and material needs, which He has promised to do.

This fourth petition is the practical consequence of the first three. Only the man who calls upon God as his Father through

Christ Jesus, who seeks His glory and His kingdom, and who above and before any personal requests wants the will of God for his own life, only such a man can continue on to pray, "Give us this day our daily bread." A relationship must be established before a request can be made.

This petition recognizes the goodness of God.

The great eternal God, the Creator of the universe and the God who is building even now an eternal kingdom, ready to be revealed at His own pleasure, knows and cares about your every need. The hairs of your head are numbered, the thoughts of your mind recorded. The Book of Isaiah says that all nations are but a drop in the bucket before God,[1] but Jesus said, "Not even a sparrow falls to the ground without your heavenly Father."[2] God is "the high and lofty one who inhabits eternity, whose name is holy" but "He dwells with him also who is of a contrite and humble spirit."[3] This great God loves, He cares. Therefore you can call upon Him for your own personal needs with the same confidence with which you also pray, "Thy kingdom come."

There are many passages in the Bible which teach us to call upon God for our material needs. With the right attitude and purpose, the Christian farmer may rightly pray for an abundant harvest, the merchant for prosperity in business, the housewife for strength to meet the demands of the home, the student for help in study. All these and many more we may pray in confidence that "my God will supply all your needs..."[4]

We must keep in mind that there are also warnings about allowing the material things to gain the upper hand. We must not allow ourselves to come under bondage to possessions. Jesus plainly warned us that the things of the kingdom must be of greatest importance to His people. Knowing this, we believe that God wants his children to trust Him and lean on His goodness for all their needs. Unless we believe that He is good and that He loves us, the words of this petition become empty and hollow mockery.

This petition recognized the dependence of man upon God.

There are no other words which express so fully, so perfectly man's complete dependence upon God. For even the most prosperous, the most secure, the most healthy, only the thin curtain of providence separates you from want and need. You may be perfectly sound of mind and body, with a secure position financially, a loving family, and the esteem and respect of your fellow man, but these things may vanish, suddenly without warning. A tragic accident, the visitation of a dread disease, a business slump, an unexpected temptation, and within hours, even moments, all earthly glory can turn to ashes in your mouth.

We forget in our complex technological society that our daily bread still comes from the processes of nature, a creation still under the control of the Creator. Our dependence upon Him is day by day, moment by moment. When Israel was in the wilderness, escaped from Egypt but not yet in the Promised Land, she was fed each day with manna from heaven. The people were instructed not to attempt to store up for the next day, but to live by faith in the goodness of God from day to day. Some disregarded God's instructions and attempted to heap up an over abundance of manna. It turned into corruption and was unfit for use. What a tremendous parable for our lives. How true it is that when we cease trusting in God and attempt to "store up" selfishly the treasures of the world we find ourselves corrupted by those very treasures. Strength for the day, that is what God promises. Bread for the day, that is what He tells us to request from Him.

We tend to think that because we have advanced in certain fields of knowledge and achievement that somehow we are no longer as dependent upon the Lord as before, but this is simply not so. We are too frail, so subject to loss, so helpless without Him. God expects and desires that you bring the needs of your life to Him. "He knows our frame, He remembers that we are dust."[5] Your heavenly Father knows you have need of these things before you ask, but it is well that you say, when you pray, "Give us this day our daily bread."

This petition recognizes the needs of all men.

This is a prayer of compassion. Jesus did not teach us to say, "Give *me my* bread," but, "Give *us our* bread." No man who is selfish can pray this prayer from his heart. To say these words in prayer one must be touched with the hunger, the needs of others. The solution to the hunger problem in our world is not primarily one of economic philosophies, or trade agreements, or even technological aid. It is first a matter of preaching the Gospel. In the very measure by which the church has pro-claimed the good news of Christ Jesus to the world, so the needs of man's physical being are brought to light, and the motivation is supplied to meet those needs. This has been true throughout the ages, and it is true today.

I think one of our great failings in this country has been that we have not been content to ask for our daily bread, but have insisted upon butter and jam to go with the bread, while so much of the rest of the world is starving. By this I mean that we have erected such a standard of high and easy living that we find ourselves isolated from the rest of the world, and untouched by its poverty. This will yet be our ruin, we worship at the altar of mammon, and in so doing we cannot also worship the true God. When we sincerely pray, "Give us this day our daily bread," we are renouncing greed and lust.

The Book of Proverbs records this simple prayer: "Give me neither poverty nor riches; feed me with my portion of nourishment, lest I be full and deny thee, and say, who is the Lord? Or lest I be poor and steal and violate God's name."[6]

> *Therefore when you pray, say,*
> *"Our Father who art in heaven,*
> *hallowed be thy name.*
> *Thy kingdom come,*
> *thy will be done,*
> *on earth, as it is in heaven.*
> *Give us this day our daily bread..."*

6

FORGIVENESS – RECEIVING AND GIVING

When you pray, "Forgive us our debts as we forgive our debtors," you are touching the heart and soul of the Christian faith, and the Christian life. This is what the Christian Gospel is all about, forgiveness. This is the secret to living the Christian life, forgiveness. These words above all help us to understand that this is a prayer for children – the children of God. If there is any lingering doubt that this is a prayer for believers only, such doubts must now end. Only the merits of the blood and righteousness of the Lord Jesus can win a sinner the right to ask for forgiveness, and only a person in whom the living Christ dwells can offer forgiveness to others.

Several years ago I heard a story that has stayed with me ever since. It was the story of a "mysterious" tombstone in a long forgotten and neglected old churchyard. There was no name, no inscription except for one word, "Forgiven." Truly this tells the story of every Christian. If this may be said of us, what more needs saying?

This petition of the Lord's Prayer is filled with the message of the Gospel, and proclaims the atonement. When you pray this prayer, your thoughts naturally turn to the cross and what Jesus did there. So let us attempt to look into this petition and grow in our understanding of what it means to pray, "Forgive us our debts as we forgive our debtors."

This petition asks for the forgiveness of our sins.

Man's greatest need is the forgiveness of his sins. Apart from this, man is truly a lost soul, without God and without hope in this world and the world to come. The good news of the Gospel centers in this greatest of all blessings, the forgiveness of sin.

There is a sense in which this is a once and for all prayer. There comes a time in every man's life when he must come to grips with the problem of sin. The circumstances may vary, but the need is the same. He may come as a publican in the temple, oppressed and overborn with such a sense of guilt that he can only beat his breast and cry out wretchedly, "God have mercy on me, the sinner." Or he may come as the rich, young ruler, knowing that something is missing, and lacking peace. Again he may come as Nicodemus, furtively, yet hungering, and seeking for relief. Sooner or later one must pray this prayer or he will never see the kingdom of God.

On the other hand, this is more than just a once and for all prayer. In writing to the believers in the early church, the Apostle John said, "If we say we have no sin, we make him (God) to be a liar, and his truth is not in us."[1] He went on to say, "If we confess our sins he is faithful and just to forgive us our sins and to cleanse us from all unrighteousness."² As children of God, we must pray this prayer if we are to walk in fellowship with Him.

Every prayer that is a Christian prayer must confess sin and unworthiness. By this petition we confess our actual transgressions, our breaking of the law. We confess our evil thoughts, our cruel and careless words, every betrayal of confidence and trust, and every denial of faith. We confess our selfish motives, our sinful outlook. We confess the deeds that are displeasing to God and harmful to our fellow man. To pray this prayer effectively, each person must go beyond these general words and confess specifically his sins to his Father in heaven.

By this petition we also confess our sins of omission and failure. We ask forgiveness for not being kind, nor concerned. We ask forgiveness for the many things we have left undone in life; our failures to love each other, our failures to bear each other's burdens, our failures to witness for Christ. Let no one ever even imagine that he has no need to pray this prayer. We all must whisper this prayer every moment. At the same time, let no one egotistically imagine that his sins are greater than God's power and love to forgive them. Despair is foolish. God will for Christ's sake forgive anyone who comes to Him. He invites you to come, He urges you to come. We have but to believe His word and come saying,

I lay my sins on Jesus,
The spotless Lamb of God,
He takes them all and frees me
From this accursed load.
I bring my guilt to Jesus
To wash my crimson stain

> *White in His blood most precious*
> *Till not a spot remain.*

This is the only way we can live in fellowship with the Lord or gain any power over sin.

We must always be careful in what spirit we come saying, "Forgive us our debts…" We must come with deep contrition and heartfelt repentance for sin, ever aware that God is not in debt to us. He doesn't have to forgive sins, but by His grace He has chosen to do so.

This petition offers forgiveness to others.

When we pray "Forgive us our debts," we follow with "As we forgive our debtors." Let us be careful first of all to notice what this does *not* say. It does not say "because we forgive our debtors." It does not say "by merit of the forgiveness of our debtors." Rather this is a gauge or test by which we may know if we have been forgiven. If we have humbled ourselves before God, confessed our sin and have been made aware of our guilt, and have been forgiven, then the forgiveness of others will follow as a result. If we have an unforgiving spirit, then we need to do some very basic re-examination of our relationship to God. The parable of the unmerciful servant as told by Christ speaks right to this point.[3] Really, if you know that you have been forgiven by the shed blood of Jesus Christ, you must forgive, you cannot help yourself or even want to. If Jesus Christ is living in you (and this is what a Christian is), your heart will not be cold and hard and unforgiving. Of course it costs to forgive. It cost God to forgive you far more than it will ever cost you to forgive another. It cost the Lord Jesus to forgive you. That's why the cross was necessary.

What should we forgive? Anything! How much, or how often? Christ's words to Simon Peter when he asked the same question deal with this.[4] This is the only petition on which Christ elaborated. He said, "For if ye forgive men not their trespasses, neither will your Heavenly Father forgive you."[5] There is something quite final and absolute about these words. True forgiveness breaks us and puts forgiveness in our hearts. Unless there is a true spirit of forgiveness in you, then when you pray this prayer the words are hollow and empty and hypocritical. The wonderful thing about forgiveness is that it sets you free to forgive, and without this freedom you are a slave indeed and can never know the meaning of true happiness or peace. If I had a worst enemy and wanted to make him miserable and it was in my power to do so, I would give him an unforgiving heart, then I know he would be miserable the rest of his life.

There is a secret to praying this prayer and meaning it. The secret, which is really no secret, is staying close to the Lord Jesus. If you live in His presence, if you let His great heart shed its warmth into your life, if you think often of Calvary, then you are given the power to do what no man can do unaided, you can forgive.

Therefore when you pray, say, "Our Father who art in heaven, hallowed by thy name. Thy kingdom come, Thy will be done on earth as it is in heaven. Give us this day our daily bread, and forgive us our debts, as we forgive our debtors."

7

LEAD US NOT INTO TEMPTATION

No Christian can ever approach the Holy God who is his Father without praying, "Forgive us our debts..." No Christian should ever be content to leave it at that, but should also always pray, "Lead us not into temptation, but deliver us from evil." In the former petition we confess our sins and ask forgiveness. In the latter we confess our weakness and ask for help and protection. These two petitions naturally follow in order. If you have experienced true repentance, if you have confessed your sins to God and have received forgiveness, then you have a holy dread of falling into sin again and grieving your Saviour. You remember what it cost to forgive, and so you wish to live a life that is pleasing to Him. Thus you pray, "Lead us not into temptation..."

This has been called a prayer for early morning. You have so many temptations of every kind facing you in this world. There is not a passing day that does not present you with opportunity and temptation to do wrong. There are temptations of the body and of the mind. There are situations to face fraught with temptation. There are people with whom you have to deal who may well lead you into compromise and error. Certainly every day should begin with this prayer.

But this is also a prayer for the "early morning" of life. Every child, every youth should have this prayer constantly on his lips and in his heart. Some may foolishly think that temptation is a good thing and that you should look for it and seek it out that you may grow strong by resisting it. Be assured that temptations, more than you can cope with, will meet you along the way. The older you grow the more you will understand the urgency of this prayer. The bird with a broken wing may fly again, but not with the same freedom, not to the same soaring heights. So we may be forgiven by God's grace, but sin still weakens and lessens our freedom and our influence for good.

This prayer is not one that should be limited to the early morning of the day or life. David warned of the "destruction that wasteth at noonday,"[1] but David forgot his own warning, and in the noontide of his life, the zenith of his strength and glory, fell into temptation and sin. Even the very old can forget to pray this prayer, and suffer because of it.

This is one of the most important and urgent requests we can ever make of God. So much depends upon it. Nothing can separate us from God and His love except our own sin. Fellowship with the Lord is the guiding light, the strength of the Christian. The "Everlasting Arms" of God's presence support and sustain. Sin intervenes and separates even a child of God from his heavenly Father. This is unbearable. So we pray, "Lead us not into temptation."

In this prayer we ask that we may not have to face dangerous temptations.

When we make this request of God, we are asking that we may not be led by our own sinful will or ignorance into situations of temptation which we cannot handle. Far too often we wait far too late to ask for help. This is one of the most common of all failures by Christians. There are times when you will be placed in peril by providence, but more often we allow ourselves to be freely led into temptation. It makes no sense to pray this prayer then pollute your mind with salacious literature and X-rated and R-rated movies. It makes no sense to pray this prayer then harbor ill will against others, allowing Satan to gain advantage over you. It makes no sense to pray this prayer then place yourself in situations of ultimate temptation and with people you know will lead you astray.

The time to think about the depth of the water is before you get in over your head and discover you can't swim. It really is foolish to put your head into the mouth of a lion and then pray that he is not hungry. If he can open his mouth _that_ wide, there is a real good chance he is hungry. Temptation is not a thing to be sought, but to be studiously, prayerfully avoided. For this we pray in this petition.

In this prayer we ask that when overtaken by temptation we may not fall.

God may allow us in our freedom and under His providence to be tempted. Job is the classic case in point of this truth. God did not tempt or afflict Job, but He allowed him to be. Little did Job understand of the cosmic significance of his suffering, or of the blessing it would be to all succeeding generations.

When we are tempted, this petition asks that we may be given wisdom to see sin for what it is and the power to resist it. It is so easy to underestimate the power of temptation and the heinousness of sin. There is never anything noble or good or insignificant about sin. If ever you get that feeling, then return once more to the cross and behold your Saviour in His agony.

Some of you undoubtedly remember the 3-D movie fad of years ago. When you went to the theatre you were given special glasses to view the film which gave the illusion of depth. Without the glasses, the screen was a fuzzy blur, and the picture unintelligible. That's the way it is with temptation and sin so often. We fail to see it in focus. By this petition we ask God to allow us to see sin in its proper perspective, so we will recognize the peril.

All of us have weak spots in our make-up. It is our duty to God and to ourselves to discover these weak points and to ask for grace to strengthen us and to shore up the fallen walls of our spiritual defenses. Samson's failing was precisely at this point. He was a great man, a strong man, but he had weaknesses that proved fatal. Even though he knew his weakness, he failed to do anything about it and placed himself deliberately in a position to fail. This we must avoid at all cost.

Basically, this is a prayer for a closer walk with Him who was tempted and tried in all points, as we are, yet without sin. Never was a man called upon to face more powerful temptations. His basic temptation was to avoid the cross. Of course, the devil wanted Him to avoid the cross, for he saw in the cross of Jesus his own downfall, and the ruin of his kingdom. Still the devil wants the cross avoided. He will do most anything to keep you from taking up your cross and following Jesus.

When we ask this petition of the Lord, we are praying that sin may not find a ready breeding ground in us. The other day I saw a service station which had been burned out because of a small spark in the wrong place. The manager was just making a routine repair of a flat tire with a "hot patch." However, the floor was covered with cleaning fluid, and when the tiny spark fell on the ready floor, a holocaust followed. So the small spark of temptation may ordinarily go unnoticed unless we have been placed in a situation of great temptation, then a deadly flame may follow.

Each act of yielding to temptation brings you one step nearer the time when you have lost your freedom not to yield.

> *When we pray this prayer, we are asking*
> *that when we are tempted and overcome*
> *that we may not be enslaved by*
> *evil or the evil one.*

"Dear Lord, when I fall prey to temptation and sin, do not let it become a way of life with me. Do not allow me, your child, to become an instrument of Satan, because I know this can happen and rob me of my reason for being. When I am hurt, do not let me become bitter or resentful. When I see evil and suffering abounding, do not allow me to become callous or careless. When I win some spiritual victory, deliver me from self-righ-

teousness. When I am too busy to pray, don't let me think I
didn't really miss much."

Remember, we do have an enemy of our souls, fierce, impla-
cable, cunning, evil. Paul reminds us, "We wrestle not against
flesh and blood, but against principalities and powers, against
spiritual wickedness in high places."[2] Because this is true we
must "put on the whole armor of God."[3] We have a Captain of
our salvation who alone has defeated and can defeat our foe.
By His cross we are saved, and by it we are encouraged when
we pray to say, "Lead us not into temptation, but deliver us
from evil."

> *Now unto Him who is able to keep you from falling*
> *And to present you faultless*
> *Before the throne of his glory with exceeding joy.*
> *To the only wise God our Savior,*
> *Be glory and majesty, dominion and power,*
> *Both now and forever. Amen.*[4]

8

THINE IS THE KINGDOM ...AMEN

The Lord's Prayer ends where it began, in heaven. It ends with the same concerns, namely the glory and the kingdom of God. All that is said before in this prayer awaits these final words. This great model prayer is really incomplete without this final ascription of faith and praise. Because we can pray these last words in faith and confident hope, we are assured that all the petitions of this prayer will be answered, and indeed all prayers. If in our prayers we are always consciously seeking the kingdom and the power and the glory of God, there is no question about their being answered.

John Calvin said that these words are given us that we might be reminded again that our prayers are grounded altogether on the goodness and power of God and not upon ourselves. The maturity of our Christian experience is measured not by the length of our prayers, nor by the zeal or despair of our petitions and requests, but rather by the amount of praise and worship we include in our prayers.

So at last we come to the final words of the Lord's Prayer. In this prayer we have been taught how to pray and for what things we are to ask. We have seen the poverty and emptiness of much of our praying. The Lord has led us into a deepening of faith and assurance. We have grown in our prayer life. Now we consider these words as a sort of grand finale, the capstone of faith and prayer.

This prayer is a great affirmation of faith.

"For thine is the kingdom and the power and the glory forever. Amen." What a daring thing it is to say these words. Only the eye of faith can see it in our troubled world. Only the voice of faith can proclaim it. By these words we declare that we believe God. We trust His word. When the Apostle Paul was speaking to the men on the sinking ship which was bearing him as a prisoner to Rome, he encouraged them with these words, "Sirs, be of good cheer, for I believe God..."[1] If there was ever a time when this same testimony needs bearing it is right now. You need to have this witness in your own life. People are so fearful and anxious. The world is in so much trouble and despair. Where are the voices of the believers saying, "Sirs, be of good cheer, for I believe God?"

We reject outright all philosophies or interpretations of history which deny or ignore the truth of God's Sovereignty.

By these words we are saying to God, "Father, we are sure of thee. Thou are trustworthy. We rest in thee as our shield and defender." To the world we are saying, "There is hope. God has a glorious and wonderful future for those who trust in Him through His Son. God lives. God rules." We invite all men to join us in this kingdom now and for all eternity.

The kingdom of God is veiled and invisible now. It is an underground movement. But not always and, we fervently believe, not for long.

> *For lo the days are hastening on*
> *By prophets long foretold,*
> *When with the ever circling years,*
> *Comes round the age of gold.*
> *When peace shall over all the earth*
> *Her ancient splendor fling,*
> *And the whole world send back the song*
> *Which now the angels sing.*

"Thine is the kingdom and the power and the glory forever." All nations and kingdoms of this world will be judged and brought to nought. "For the things which are seen are temporal."[2] God's kingdom shall be all in all. It shall never end. "The things which are not now seen are eternal."[3]

This prayer is an act of dedication and commitment.

No one can truly pray this prayer who does not face up to the commitment it implies. It is no good at all to have mental reservations when you pray this prayer. "Thine is the kingdom so long as I have my own way and am happy. Thine is the kingdom, but don't expect me to tell anyone about it or how to enter it. Thine is the kingdom, but I'm much too busy to do anything about it. Thine is the kingdom, but what's mine is mine, and don't expect me to tithe." You see how foolish and sinful it is to say these words insincerely?

Praying this prayer is taking your life in your hands and placing it in the hands of your heavenly Father to do with and to use as He pleases. Don't be mistaken at this point. You do have an active role to play. Your faith alone can unlock the door to God's kingdom and power and glory in your life.

One day Jesus returned to the place where He grew up to teach in the synagogue. Matthew tells us that He did not do many mighty works there because of their unbelief.[4] The same thing is true today. Unbelief can and will prevent the blessing of God in your life. When you say these words in prayer, you are crowning the Lord Jesus as your King, and you are placing all you are and have at His disposal.

In medieval times, when some lord or baron would pledge fealty to a king, he was placing his wealth, his honor, his servants, and his all at the feet of the king for his service. When we make this act of dedication in prayer, we are doing something total and final and irrevocable.

This prayer raises life's most important question.

The word "forever" raises and important question, the most important question of all. Before you can personally add the final "amen" to this prayer, you must face and deal with the question this prayer raises. Where will you spend that "forever?" Where will you spend eternity? You will never face a more urgent, relevant question. We may pray every day, "Thine is the kingdom and power and glory forever," but it takes more than just saying these words to insure a place in that grand "forever." There is only one way. You must come to God in confession of sin, deep and heartfelt. You must repent, turning from your sin and seeking forgiveness. You must accept within your heart Jesus Christ and what He has done for you on the cross. Then and only then are the final words of this prayer a comfort.

The last word of this prayer is "amen," which simply means, "so be it," or "it is true;" or when personally applied it means, "I believe." How can you add your own final "amen" to this prayer? By taking Christ into your heart. By learning the lessons of trust and obedience. By a life yielded and filled with the Holy Spirit. By learning to be a good steward of all that God has entrusted in your care, your money, your time, your opportunities and abilities. In fact your whole life should be a grand amen to the Lord's Prayer.

Therefore when you pray say;
Our Father, which art in heaven,
Hallowed be thy Name.
Thy Kingdom come.
Thy will be done in earth,
As it is in heaven.
Give us this day our daily bread.
And forgive us our trespasses,
As we forgive them that trespass against us.
And lead us not into temptation,
But deliver us from evil.
For thine is the kingdom,
The power, and the glory,
For ever and ever.
Amen.

REFERENCES

Introduction

1. Matthew 6:6
2. Matthew 7:7

Increasing Your Faith

1. John 7:6
2. John 8:44
3. Psalm 103:12
4. Micah 7:19
5. Hebrews 4:13
6. Ephesians 3:20

Hallowed Be Thy Name

1. Psalm 34:3
2. Isaiah 6
3. Philippians 2:11

Thy Kingdom Come

1. Matthew 6:33
2. Mark 1:15
3. Luke 23:42-43
4. Matthew 18:3
5. II Corinthians 4:4
6. II Peter 3:12
7. Mark 14:25

Thy Will be Done in Earth as it is in Heaven

1. Habakkuk 2:4
2. Luke 22:39-46

Give Us this Day our Daily Bread

1. Isaiah 40:15
2. Matthew 10:29
3. Isaiah 57:15
4. Philippians 4:19
5. Psalm 103:14
6. Proverbs 30:8, 9

Forgiveness – Receiving and Giving

1. I John 1:10
2. I John 1:9
3. Matthew 18:23ff.
4. Matthew 18:21-22
5. Matthew 6:14-15

Lead Us Not into Temptation

1. Psalm 91:6
2. Ephesians 6:12
3. Ephesians 6:13
4. Jude 24-25

Thine is the Kingdom . . . Amen

1. Acts 27:25
2. II Corinthians 4:18
3. II Corinthians 4:18
4. Matthew 13:58

OUR FATHER,

WHICH ART IN HEAVEN,

HALLOWED BE THY NAME.

THY KINGDOM COME.

THY WILL BE DONE IN EARTH,

AS IT IS IN HEAVEN.

GIVE US THIS DAY OUR DAILY BREAD.

AND FORGIVE US OUR TRESPASSES,

AS WE FORGIVE THEM THAT TRESPASS AGAINST US.

AND LEAD US NOT INTO TEMPTATION,

BUT DELIVER US FROM EVIL.

FOR THINE IS THE KINGDOM,

THE POWER, AND THE GLORY,

for ever and ever, Amen.

www.ingramcontent.com/pod-product-compliance
Lightning Source LLC
LaVergne TN
LVHW051203080426
835508LV00021B/2780